It's Tattling, Anita!

Text and photos by Carolina Cisneros

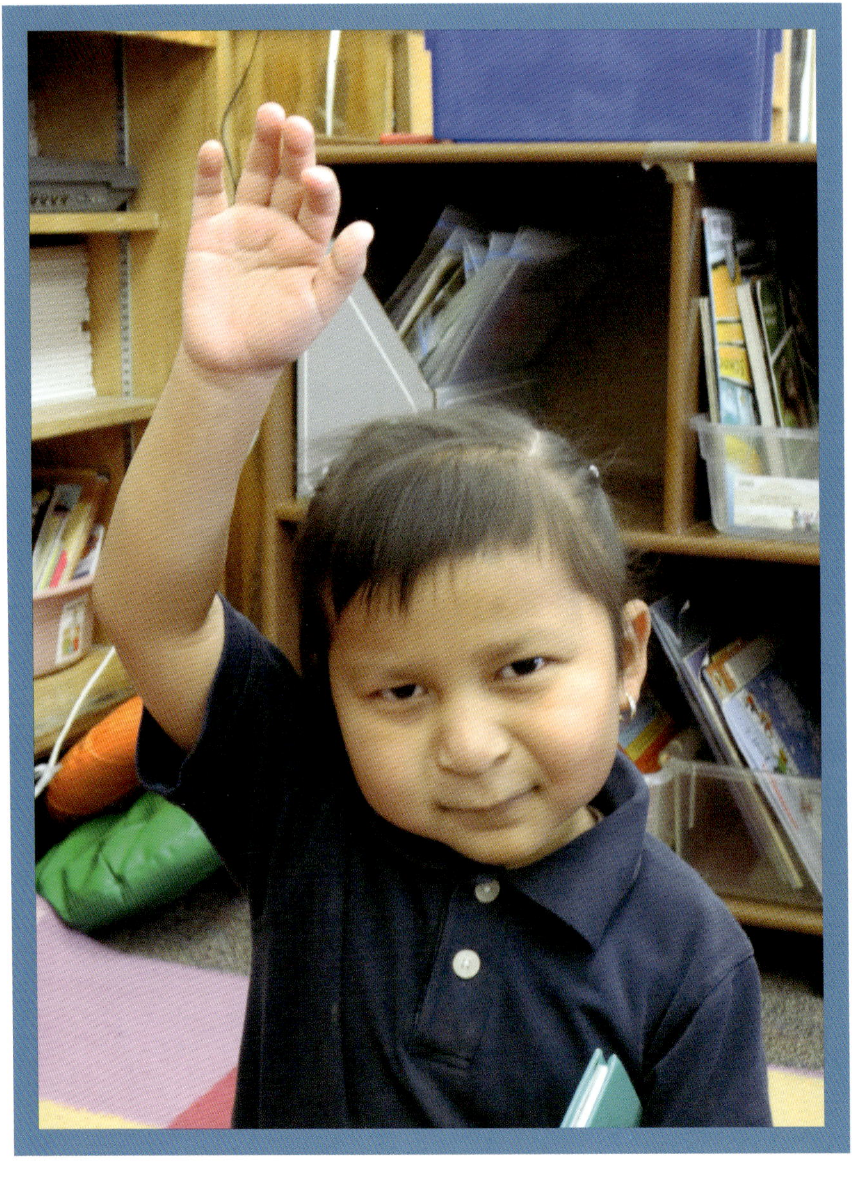

Anita was a big tattletale who liked to get involved in everybody's problems. She tattled so much that the other kids called her "Anita the Tattletale." She always complained to the teacher.

"Teacher, Joseph stuck his tongue out at me," complained Anita.

"Teacher, Diana didn't finish her homework," tattled Anita.

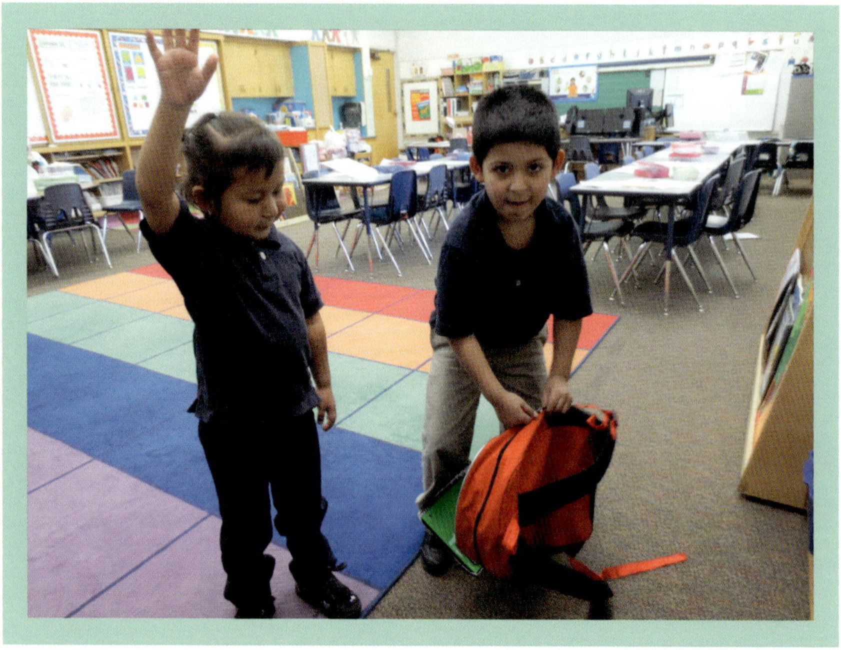

"Teacher, Marco put his notebook into his backpack before he finished his work," complained Anita.

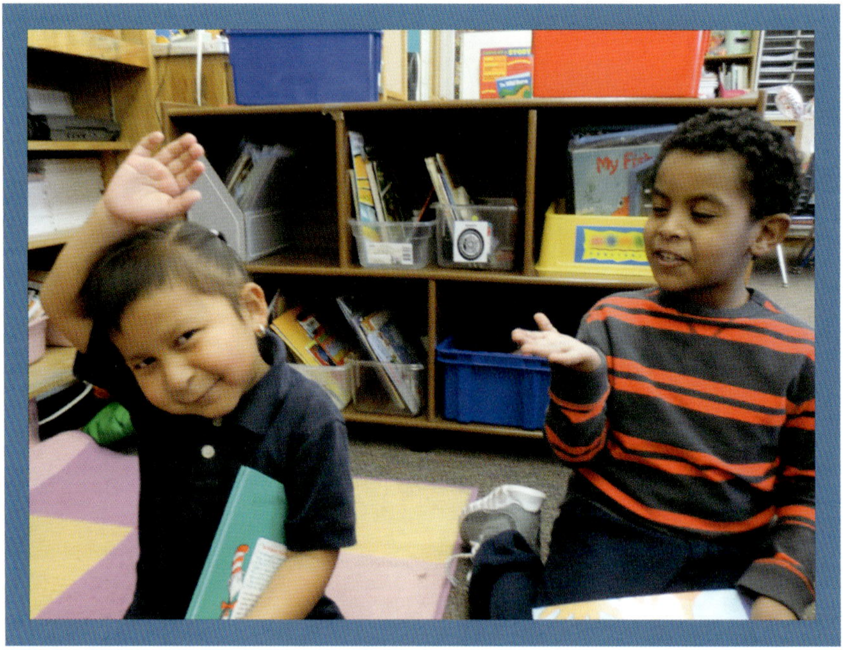
My Fish

"Teacher, Eben blew me a kiss!" tattled Anita.

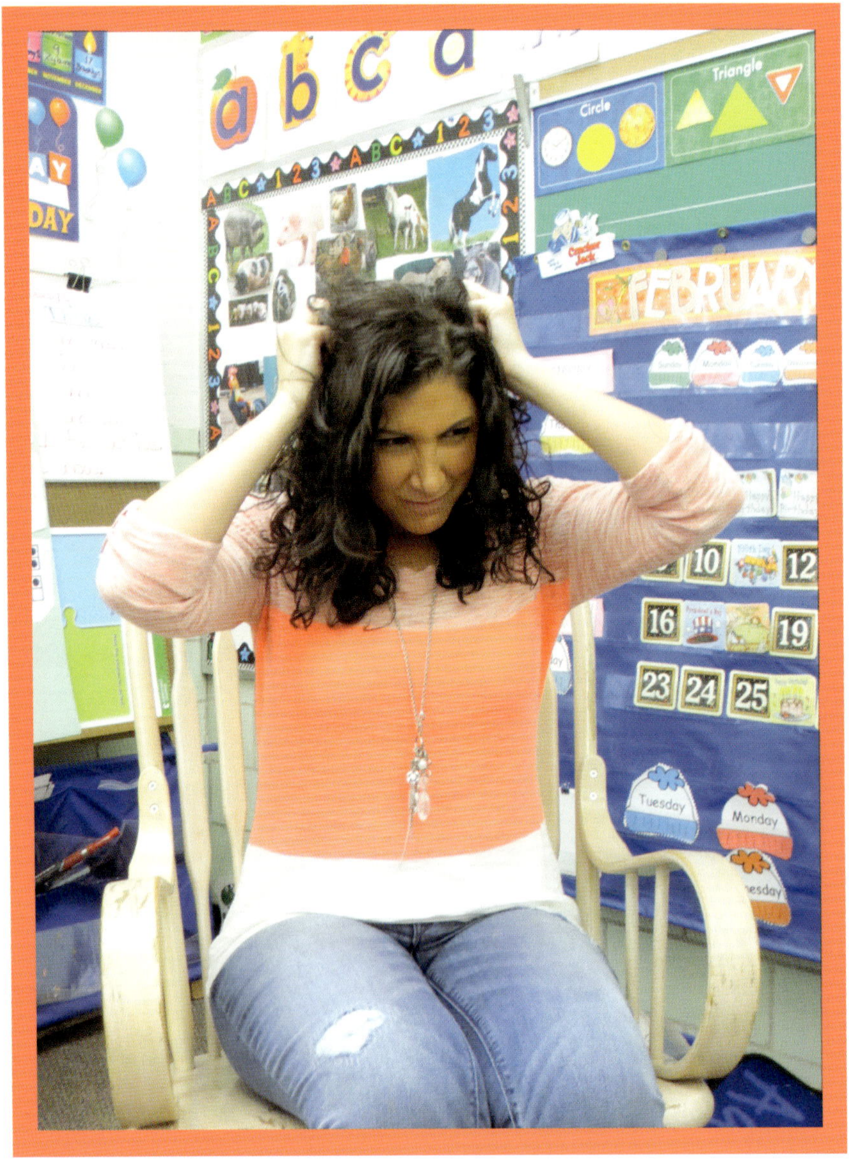
Circle
Triangle
Tuesday
Monday

The teacher was tired of hearing all of Anita's complaints. She thought to herself, "I'm going to explain to the class the difference between tattling and telling because I am tired of so much tattling!"

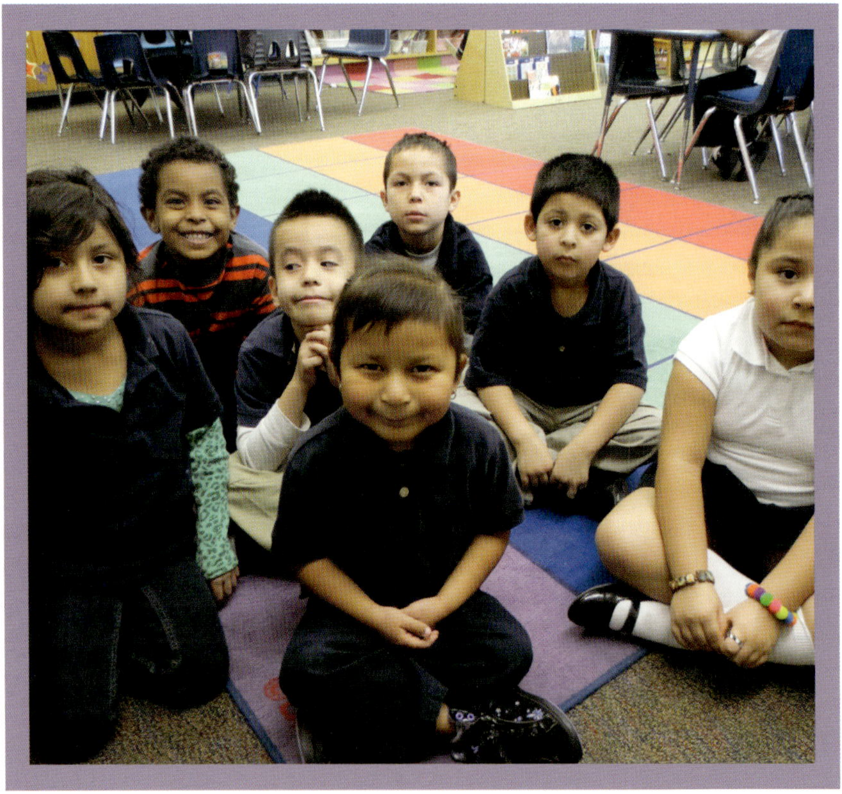

The teacher called all the children together and had them sit on the rug.

14

"Children," she began, "Tattling is when you tell the teacher what other people are doing just because you want to get them in trouble. Can anyone give me some examples?"

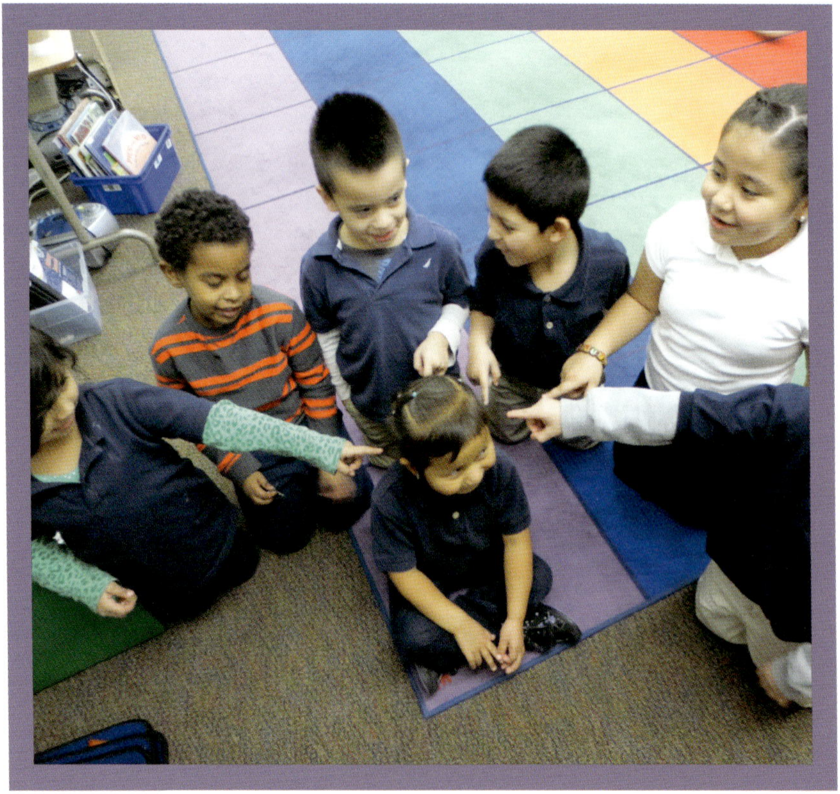

All of the children looked at Anita. Her cheeks turned bright red.

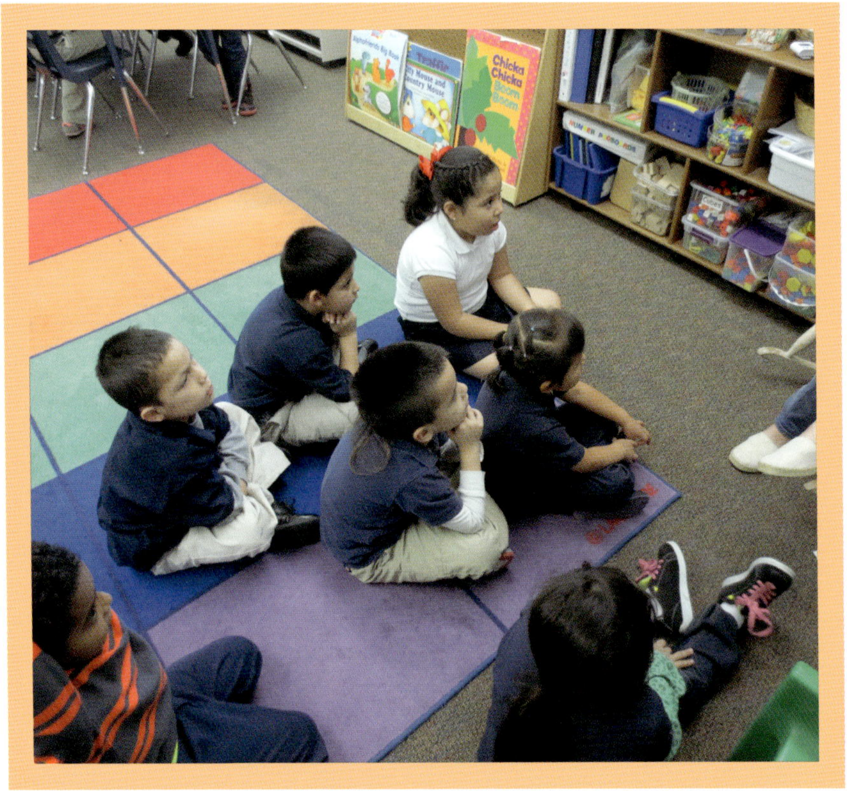
Chicka Chicka Boom Boom

"Telling the teacher is something you should do when another student is doing something that is dangerous that could hurt someone or damage something. Do you understand the difference?" asked the teacher.

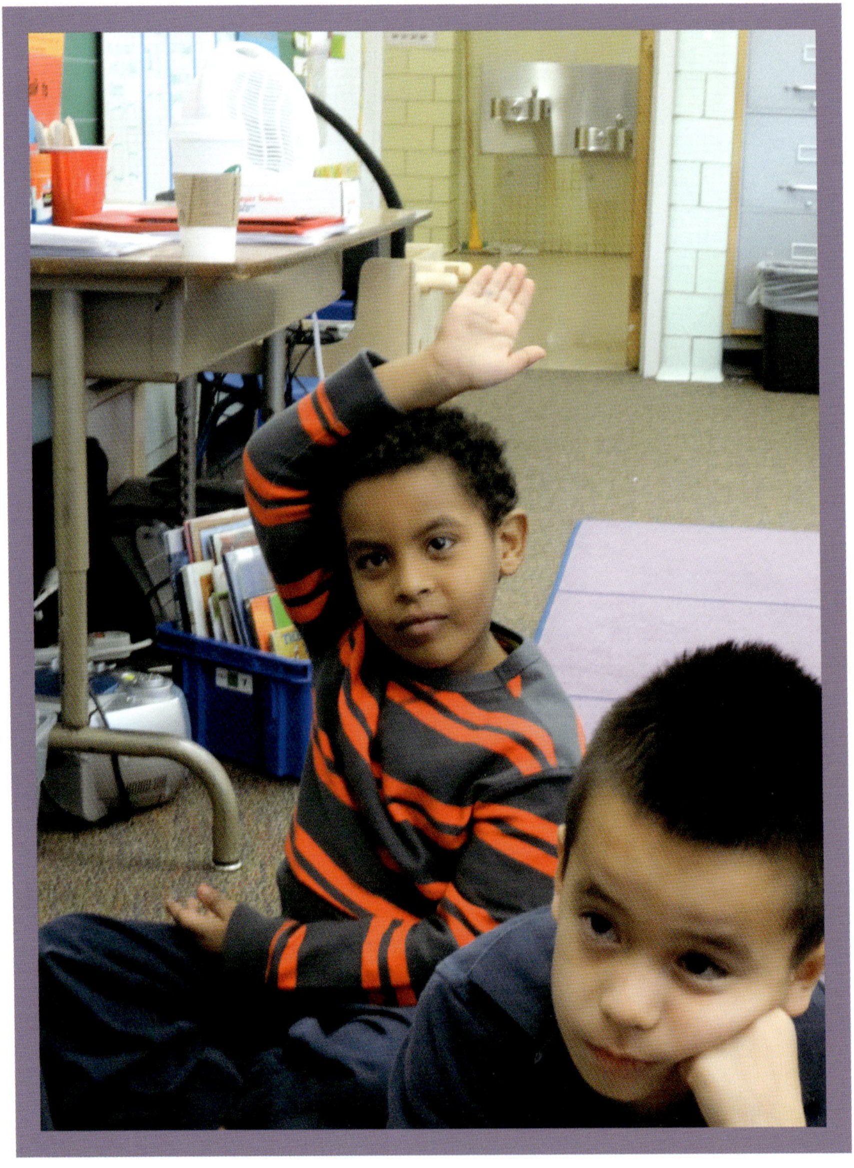

Eben raised his hand. "Not really, Teacher."

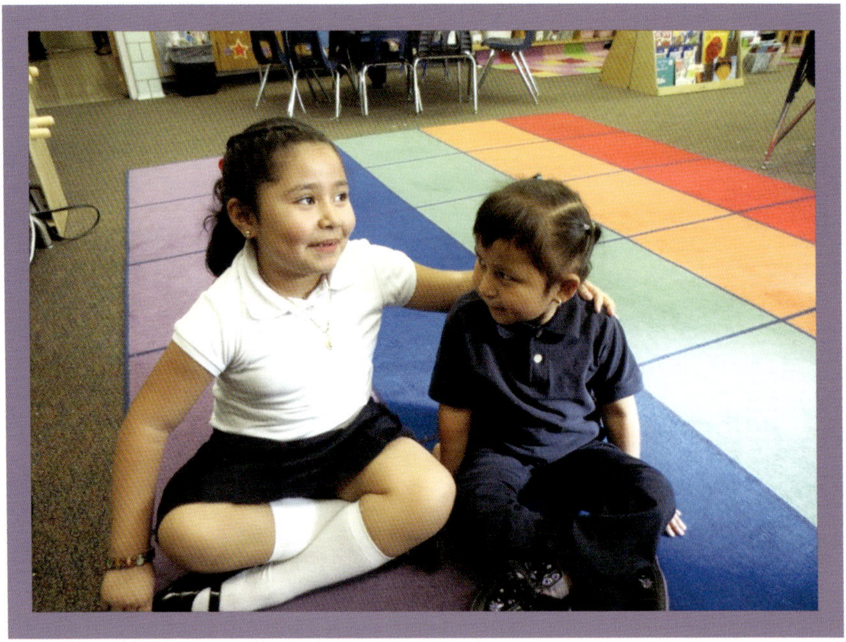

"I do," said Diana. "If you see something dangerous, you should tell the teacher. If you see someone throw a rock at another person, you should tell the teacher. Or if someone pushes you or says bad words and you feel afraid, you should tell."

"Very good, Diana. When you see something dangerous, you should report it to the teacher. But if not ..."

"It's tattling!" yelled all the students, including Anita.